PRESENTED TO

ON THE OCCASION OF

FROM

DATE

A LITTLE INSPIRATION

FOR A *Hope* FILLED DAY

BARBOUR
PUBLISHING

© 2003 by Barbour Publishing, Inc.

ISBN 1-59310-229-1

Compiled by Connie Troyer, Jessica Owens, and Kelly Williams.

Published by Barbour Publishing, Inc., P.O. Box 719, Uhrichsville, Ohio 44683, www.barbourbooks.com

*Our mission is to publish and distribute inspirational products offering exceptional value
and biblical encouragement to the masses.*

Member of the
Evangelical Christian
Publishers Association

Printed in China.
5 4 3 2 1

Men and women are limited
not by the place of their birth,
not by the color of their skin,
but by the size of their hope.

JOHN JOHNSON

True hope dwells on the possible,
even when life seems to be a plot written by
someone who wants to
see how much adversity we can overcome.

WALTER ANDERSON

The Confidence Course:
Seven Steps to Self-Fulfillment

Life affords no higher pleasure than
that of surmounting difficulties,
passing from one step of success to another,
forming new wishes, and seeing them gratified.
He that labors in any great or laudable undertaking
has his fatigues first supported by hope,
and afterwards rewarded by joy. . . .
To strive with difficulties, and to conquer them,
is the highest human felicity.

SAMUEL JOHNSON

Light from Many Lamps

Hope can come from having a good day.

EMILIE BARNES

We must accept finite disappointment,
but never lose infinite hope.

MARTIN LUTHER KING JR.

The very least you can do in your life
is to figure out what you hope for.
And the most you can do
is live inside that hope.

BARBARA KINGSOLVER

Life with Christ is an endless hope,
without Him a hopeless end.

ANONYMOUS

Hope is not the conviction that
something will turn out well,
but the certainty that
something makes sense regardless of
how it turns out.

VACLAV HAVEL

I place no hope in my strength,
nor in my works:
but all my confidence is in God my protector,
who never abandons those who have
put all their hope and thought in Him.

FRANÇOIS RABELAIS

What means the fact—which is so common,
so universal—that some soul that has lost
all hope for itself can inspire in another
listening soul an infinite confidence in it,
even while it is expressing its despair?

HENRY DAVID THOREAU

Be strong and take heart,
all you who hope in the LORD.

PSALM 31:24 NIV

Hope, like faith,

is nothing if it is not courageous.

THORNTON WILDER

Whatever enlarges hope
will also exalt courage.

SAMUEL JOHNSON

One of the best safeguards of our hopes,
I have suggested, is to be able to
mark off the areas of hopelessness
and to acknowledge them,
to face them directly,
not with despair but with
the creative intent of keeping them from
polluting all the areas of possibility.

WILLIAM F. LYNCH

It is certainly wrong to despair;
and if despair is wrong, hope is right.

SIR JOHN LUBBOCK

Because you live, O Christ,
the spirit bird of hope is freed for flying,
our cages of despair no longer keep us
closed and life-denying.

SHIRLEY ERENA MURRAY
"Because You Live, O Christ"

We grow great by dreams. All big men are dreamers. They see things in the soft haze of a spring day or in the red fire of a long winter's evening. Some of us let these great dreams die, but others nourish and protect them; nurse them through bad days till they bring them to the sunshine and light, which comes always to those who sincerely hope that their dreams will come true.

WOODROW WILSON

Hope is wanting something so eagerly that—
in spite of all the evidence that
you're not going to get it—
you go right on wanting it.

NORMAN VINCENT PEALE

Hope is putting faith to work
when doubting would be easier.

AUTHOR UNKNOWN

Hope, like the gleaming taper's light,
Adorns and cheers our way;
And still, as darker grows the night,
Emits a brighter ray.

OLIVER GOLDSMITH
The Captivity, Act ii

You will be secure,
because there is hope.

JOB 11:18 NIV

Hope never abandons you.

GEORGE WEINBERG

My soul, wait only upon God
and silently submit to Him;
for my hope and expectation are from Him. . . .
Trust in, lean on, rely on, and have confidence in Him
at all times, you people;
pour out your hearts before Him.
God is a refuge for us
(a fortress and a high tower).

PSALM 62:5, 8 AMP

Hope is the thing with feathers—
That perches in the soul—
And sings the tune without the words—
And never stops—at all—

EMILY DICKINSON

Don't lose hope.

When it gets darkest the stars come out.

AUTHOR UNKNOWN

Eternity is the divine treasure house,

and hope is the window,

by means of which

mortals are permitted to see,

as through a glass darkly,

the things which God is preparing.

If God hath made this world so fair,
Where sin and death abound,
How beautiful beyond compare
Will paradise be found!

JAMES MONTGOMERY

There is hope for the future.
When the world is ready for a new and better life
all this will some day come to pass
in God's good time.

20,000 Leagues Under the Sea

Beyond this vale of tears
There is a life above,
Unmeasured by the flight of years;
And all that life is love.

JAMES MONTGOMERY

Everything that is done in the world
is done by hope.
No husbandman would sow
one grain of corn if he hoped not
it would grow up and become seed;
no bachelor would marry a wife if
he hope not to have children;
no merchant or tradesman would set himself to work
if he did not hope to reap benefit thereby.

MARTIN LUTHER

Hope is the feeling we have
that the feeling we have is not permanent.

MIGNON McLAUGHLIN

Such is hope, heaven's own gift to
struggling mortals, pervading,
like some subtle essence from the skies,
all things both good and bad.

CHARLES DICKENS

We know that all things work together
for good to them that love God.

ROMANS 8:28 KJV

Faith goes up the stairs that love has built
and looks out the window
which hope has opened.

CHARLES SPURGEON

Hope is
faith holding out its hand in the dark.

GEORGE ILES

Optimism is the faith that
leads to achievement.
Nothing can be done
without hope or confidence.

HELEN KELLER

We can walk without fear, full of hope
and courage and strength...
waiting for the endless good which
God is always giving as fast as He can
get us to take it in.

GEORGE MACDONALD

I steer my bark with Hope
in the head,
leaving Fear astern.

THOMAS JEFFERSON

Do not look forward to the changes
and chances of this life in fear;
rather look to them with full hope that,
as they arise, God, whose you are,
will deliver you out of them.

ST. FRANCIS DE SALES

There is surely a future hope for you,
and your hope will not be cut off.

PROVERBS 23:18 NIV

"For I know the plans I have for you,"
declares the LORD, "plans to prosper you
and not to harm you,
plans to give you hope and a future."

JEREMIAH 29:11 NIV

Each of us enters the world because
hope for the future preceded us.

MARGE KENNEDY

*100 Things You Can Do
to Keep Your Family Together*

Hope is itself a species of happiness.

SAMUEL JOHNSON

Practice hope.

As hopefulness becomes a habit,

you can achieve a permanently happy spirit.

NORMAN VINCENT PEALE
Positive Thinking Every Day

Happiness is something to do,
something to love,
something to hope for.

CHINESE PROVERB

Of all ills that one endures,
hope is a cheap and universal cure.

ABRAHAM COWLEY

Hope is necessary in every condition.
The miseries of poverty,
sickness, and captivity would,
without this comfort,
be insupportable.

SAMUEL JOHNSON

The human body experiences a powerful
gravitational pull in the direction of hope.
That is why the patient's hopes are
the physician's secret weapon.
They are the hidden ingredients
in any prescription.

The best we can hope for in this life is
a knothole peek at
the shining realities ahead.
Yet a glimpse is enough.
It's enough to convince our hearts that
whatever sufferings and sorrows
currently assail us aren't worthy of
comparison to that which
waits over the horizon.

JONI EARECKSON TADA

Anyone who is among the living has hope.

ECCLESIASTES 9:4 NIV

Hope floods my heart with delight!
Running on air, mad with life, dizzy, reeling,
Upward I mount—faith is sight, life is feeling,
Hope is the day-star of might!

MARGARET WITTER FULLER
Dryad Song, Stanza 1

May the God of your hope so fill you
with all joy and peace in believing
[through the experience of your faith]
that by the power of the Holy Spirit you may
abound and be overflowing (bubbling over)
with hope.

ROMANS 15:13 AMP

The joy that comes past hope
and beyond expectation is like
no other pleasure in extent.

SOPHOCLES

Hope springs exulting on triumphant wing.

ROBERT BURNS

So long as faith with freedom reigns

And loyal hope survives,

And gracious charity remains

To leaven lowly lives;

While there is one untrodden tract

For intellect or will,

And men are free to think and act,

Life is worth living still.

ALFRED AUSTIN

"Is Life Worth Living?"

Life without hope is an empty,
boring, and useless life.
I cannot imagine that I could strive for
something if I did not carry hope in me.
I am thankful to God for this gift.
It is as big as life itself.

VACLAV HAVEL

While there is life there's hope,
he cried.

JOHN GAY

We live by
admiration, hope, and love.

WILLIAM WORDSWORTH

I live on hope, and that I think do all
who come into this world.

ROBERT SEYMOUR BRIDGES

Hope is
a necessity for normal life.

KARL A. MENNINGER

Time is a great teacher;
Who can live without hope?

CARL SANDBURG

If it were not for hopes,
the heart would break.

THOMAS FULLER

Hope is like a harebell
trembling from its birth.

CHRISTINA GEORGINA ROSSETTI

No winter lasts forever;
no spring skips its turn.

HAL BORLAND

Sometimes our fate resembles
a fruit tree in winter.
Who would think that those branches
would turn green again and blossom,
but we hope it, we know it.

Johann Wolfgang von Goethe

Sometimes when we've run out of hope,
what we've really run out of is patience.

EMILIE BARNES

Hope is patiently waiting expectantly for
the intangible to become reality.

AVERY D. MILLER

Hope begins in the dark,
the stubborn hope that if you just show up
and try to do the right thing,
the dawn will come.
You wait and watch and work:
you don't give up.

ANNE LAMOTT

When we have hope,
we are showing that we trust God
to work out the situation.

BARBARA JOHNSON

Hope is always available to us.
When we feel defeated,
we need only take a deep breath and say,
"Yes," and hope will reappear.

MONROE FORESTER

Let perseverance be your engine
and hope your fuel.

H. JACKSON BROWN JR.

When the world says, "Give up,"

Hope whispers, "Try it one more time."

AUTHOR UNKNOWN

Hope is like a road in the country;

there was never a road,

but when many people walk on it,

the road comes into existence.

LIN YUTANG

Most of the important things
in the world have been accomplished by
people who have kept on trying
when there seemed to be no hope at all.

DALE CARNEGIE

Hope to the end.

1 PETER 1:13 KJV

Hope against hope,
and ask till ye receive.

Expect to have hope rekindled.
Expect your prayers to be answered
in wondrous ways.
The dry seasons in life do not last.
The spring rains will come again.

SARAH BAN BREATHNACH

A friend is
the hope of the heart.

RALPH WALDO EMERSON

Every parent is at some time
the father of the unreturned prodigal,
with nothing to do but
keep his house open to hope.

John Ciardi

What would it mean to live
in a city whose people were changing
each other's despair into hope?—
You yourself must change it.

ADRIENNE RICH
"Dreams Before Waking"
Your Native Land, Your Life

There is hope for a tree:
If it is cut down, it will sprout again,
and its new shoots will not fail.
Its root may grow old in the ground,
and its stump die in the soil,
yet at the scent of water it will bud
and put forth shoots like a plant.

JOB 14:7–9 NIV

Why art thou cast down,
O my soul?
and why art thou disquieted
within me?
hope thou in God:
for I shall yet praise him,
who is the health of my countenance,
and my God.

PSALM 42:11 KJV

Hope springs eternal
in the human breast.

ALEXANDER POPE

The strongest people aren't
always the people who win,
but the people who don't give up
when they lose.

ASHLEY HODGESON

But those who hope in the LORD
will renew their strength.

ISAIAH 40:31

Hope means hoping when things are hopeless,
or it is no virtue at all. . . .
As long as matters are really hopeful,
hope is mere flattery or platitude;
it is only when everything is hopeless
that hope begins to be a strength.

G. K. CHESTERTON

Of all the forces that
make for a better world,
none is so indispensable,
none so powerful, as hope.

CHARLES SAWYER

Hope, the patent medicine
For disease, disaster, sin.

WALLACE RICE

In the dark dreary nights,
when the storm is at its most fierce,
the lighthouse burns bright so
the sailors can find their way home again.
In life the same light burns.
This light is fueled with love, faith, and hope.
And through life's most fierce storms
these three burn their brightest so
we also can find our way home again.

AUTHOR UNKNOWN

Do not let your fire go out, spark by irreplaceable spark,

in the hopeless swamps of the approximate,

the not-quite, the not-yet, the not-at-all.

Do not let the hero in your soul perish,

in lonely frustration for the life you deserved,

but have never been able to reach.

Check your road and the nature of your battle.

The world you desired can be won.

It exists, it is real, it is possible, it is yours.

AYN RAND

Never talk defeat.
Use words like
hope, belief, faith, victory.

NORMAN VINCENT PEALE
Positive Thinking Every Day

Hope is a vigorous principle. . .
it sets the head and heart to work,
and animates a man to do his utmost.

JEREMY COLLIER